Sugar Inspirations

Cake Top Ornaments

MARK RICHARDS

MEREHURST

Dedication

To my wife and best friend Sandra, for all your love and support,
as well as making the flowers, doing all the typing....

Published 1995 by Merehurst Limited
Ferry House, 51–57 Lacy Road, Putney,
London SW15 1PR

Copyright © Merehurst Limited 1995
ISBN 1-85391-494-0

A catalogue record for this book is available from the
British Library.

Editor: Helen Southall
Design: Anita Ruddell
Photography by Alan Marsh

Colour separation by P & W Graphics Pty Ltd, Singapore
Printed in Italy by Milanostampa SpA

Contents

Introduction

Simple or elaborate, sugar cake top ornaments add character and charm to celebration cakes of all kinds, and make excellent keepsakes.

It has long been traditional to finish a celebration cake with an ornament befitting the occasion – a vase of fresh flowers, a porcelain bride and groom, even a plastic stork. Increasingly, these ornaments have been made of sugar, often specially designed to give a more personal touch to the cake decoration.

One of the beauties of these edible ornaments is that they can be saved as a keepsake, a lasting memento of a happy occasion. Another advantage is that they can be pre-pared in advance – ideal for that last-minute order.

This book shows you how to create sugar cake top ornaments for numerous occasions, from birthdays and Christenings to Christmas and retirement. Some of the ornaments are truly versatile: a few small changes to the basic design and a cake top for a man's birthday is transformed into a keepsake for a Mother's Day cake. A number of simple cake designs are included to give you ideas for presenting the ornaments.

I hope you will enjoy creating the designs in this book: I have tried to include something for everyone, from the absolute beginner to the more experienced enthusiast.

Tools and Equipment

The following is a list of the items you will need to make the cake ornaments in this book. Many of the items are standard kitchen equipment; the others are easily obtainable from general cookware or specialist cake decorating shops.

Specialist tools

Ball tool
Bone tool
Dresden tool
Nylon rolling pin and board
Basketweave rolling pin
Edible glue (bought or home-made)
Plaque cutters
Thin plastic or perspex spacers
Heart cutters
Various plunger cutters
Selection of piping tubes (tips)

Basic equipment

Scissors (fine)
Cocktail sticks (toothpicks)
Icing (confectioner's) sugar and/or white fat (shortening) for marzipan (almond paste) work
Cornflour and/or white fat (shortening) for pastillage/mexican paste work
Sharp kitchen knife and/or craft knife or scalpel
Palette knife (preferably cranked)
Paintbrushes
Pizza cutting wheel or rolling wheel paper cutter
Rice paper
Food colourings
Greaseproof paper (parchment)
Cardboard roll from centre of absorbent kitchen paper

Using Modelling Tools

Ball tool This is used for making depressions, such as eye sockets, or for cupping small pieces of paste to form, for instance, ears or leaves.

Bone tool This can be used in the same way as a ball tool, but it is also useful for smoothing joins between sections of paste, and for creating broad grooves to give, for instance, the effect of pleating. It can also be used to thin the edge of the paste.

Dresden tool This is sharp at one end and blunt at the other. The sharp or veining end is used for scoring paste, making small pinpricks and for rolling paste. The broad end is used for scoring, and for making oval depressions and grooves. It is also useful for frilling and fluting.

Paste Techniques

Cake ornaments are best made from mexican paste or pastillage because these pastes dry to a smooth, hard finish. Recipes for both pastes are on page 42.

Colouring
Mexican paste and pastillage are usually coloured with droplet (liquid) or paste food colouring. Paste colours are more suitable for very dark colours as they do not soften the paste as much as the liquid colourings. Add the colour to the paste in tiny amounts (with a cocktail stick/toothpick if using a paste colour). Knead the paste thoroughly to work the colour in, if necessary adding more colour until you have the required

shade. If the paste is too dark, then knead in a little more white paste. Put the paste in a plastic bag and allow to stand for 10–20 minutes to firm up again.

You can use dusting powders to colour paste, but to do this you must mix the dry powder with some white fat (shortening) to form a paste. Add this to the mexican or pastillage paste and knead in thoroughly as described above. If you add dusting powder without mixing it with fat, the paste will take on a speckled appearance – ideal if you want to make a freckled face!

Rolling Out

A nylon pin and board are best for rolling out mexican paste or pastillage. Use a smooth rolling action to avoid producing ridges and grooves in the paste. If you need a sheet of even thickness, such as for making the back of a card, use thin plastic or perspex spacers. Before rolling, dust the board lightly with icing (confectioner's) sugar or cornflour. Use a dredger or herb shaker for icing (confectioner's) sugar, but for cornflour it is easier to make a dusting bag by tying some cornflour in a small piece of muslin.

Alternatively, you can grease the board with white fat (shortening) by smearing a very thin film of fat over the board with a fingertip. Rolling on white fat (shortening) helps prevent the paste drying too quickly.

Cutting

Transfer the paste to a piece of formica, or lift it and turn the board over so that cutting is done on the reverse side of the board. Never use the top surface of the board for cutting, especially if using a craft knife or scalpel, as this would create fine cuts in the surface of the board which would mark any paste rolled out on it in the future. Cuts in the surface would also make paste more likely to stick. A smear of white fat (shortening) under the paste will reduce drag (as will a sharp knife) and prevent it slipping, enabling you to cut shapes more accurately.

After cutting the shape required, ease it carefully off the board with a cranked palette knife, taking care not to distort the shape. Place on a surface lightly dusted with cornflour and leave to dry.

Drying

As a general rule, leave pieces to dry for 24 hours, turning once. As sections dry, exposed

areas will turn a lighter shade than other areas, such as the surface that is in contact with the board. When the paste is an even shade all over it is dry.

The drying time can be reduced by placing the pieces on a sponge. This will allow air to circulate underneath as well as on top. Airing cupboards can also be used, but take care not to dry pieces too quickly as they are more likely to warp. This is because the paste shrinks slightly as it dries. If a sheet of paste is dried so that the top surface dries much more quickly than the underside, the corners will turn up. Turning the paste over helps reverse this trend.

Plaques

As well as being decorative in themselves, plaques also make ideal bases for ornaments. They can be made in an endless variety of shapes, using either templates or cutters, and can be decorated using texturing techniques.

Templates

Templates are easy to make and easy to use. They can be made from plastic, such as margarine lids; from thin card, such as an empty breakfast cereal packet; or even from the thin metal used to make drinks cans. Plastic and aluminium can be washed. For best results, follow these simple tips:

* Cut a small 'V' shape in the centre of the template and lift the flap up – this will provide a convenient handle for removing the template from the paste.

* Keep templates clean and flat – a ring binder with plastic sleeves is ideal for this.

* To avoid jagged edges, use a smooth action when cutting around templates, especially along straight lines.

* On exposed corners, overcut each side as this will produce a neater finish. On internal corners, cut from the corner outwards.

* A pizza cutting wheel or a rolling wheel paper cutter can be used as an alternative to a craft knife or scalpel, especially when cutting long straight sections. The rolling action of the wheel reduces paste drag.

Cutters

A wide range of plaque cutters is available, including round, oval, scalloped oval, square and Garrett frill cutters. Plain and fluted scone cutters can also be used.

* When using a cutter, roll the paste out on a surface dusted with icing (confectioner's) sugar or cornflour (not white fat/shortening).

* Press the cutter down firmly, then move it in a circular motion to obtain a clean cut. Take away the excess paste.

* Trim away any remaining excess paste around the edge of the plaque using a craft knife.

Texturing

Various techniques for texturing plaques are used in the designs in this book. A number of these are described below:

Embossing

Commercial embossers or buttons can give a delightful edging to a plaque or can be used to produce an overall effect. When dry, the embossed patterns can be dusted and/or painted if wished.

Frilling

A soft, lightly frilled edge to a plaque can be produced by rolling a cocktail stick (toothpick) around the edge. Lightly dust the edges to give added effect.

Ribbed/basketweave rollers

These will give a neat, even pattern all over a plaque. Cut out the plaque after you have textured the paste.

Paper doilies

Place a doily on a sheet of paste lightly dusted with cornflour. Roll over with a rolling pin to produce a delicate embossed pattern in the paste.

Spray Holders

These attractive holders are ideal for holding sprays of flowers at different levels without the need for inserting anything into the cake.

Round Cup

Materials

60g (2oz) mexican paste/pastillage (see page 42)
Edible glue or water

Equipment

5cm (2 inch) plain round cutter
3.5cm (1½ inch) long petal cutter, such as a clematis cutter
Paintbrush

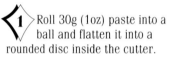

1 Roll 30g (1oz) paste into a ball and flatten it into a rounded disc inside the cutter.

2 Roll 15g (½oz) paste into a sausage shape and form into a circle on top of the disc. While still soft, make a depression in the top of the disc to take the flowers.

3 Roll out the remaining paste, cut out six petals and attach around the holder with glue. Leave to dry.

Short Stand

Materials

45g (1½oz) mexican paste/pastillage (see page 42)
Edible glue or water

Equipment

All-in-one rose or blossom cutter
Ball tool
Paintbrush
Calyx cutter

1 Roll out some paste and cut out the base of the stand using an all-in-one five-petalled rose or blossom cutter. Soften the edges of the petals using the ball tool, gently curving the petals upwards.

2 Roll a cylinder of paste 3.5cm (1½ inches) long with a diameter of 1cm (½ inch) at one end, tapering to 0.5cm (¼ inch) at the other end.

3 Open up the narrow end using the ball tool to create a well 1.5cm (¾ inch) deep. Allow to dry.

4 Fix the stem of the holder on to the base. Allow to dry. Roll out the remaining paste and cut out a calyx. Fix to the top of the holder and make a hole in the centre. Allow to dry.

Vase

Materials

60g (2oz) mexican paste/pastil-lage (see page 42)
Hollyberry and liquorice food colourings
Edible glue or water

Equipment

5cm (2 inch) round cutter
Embosser (optional)
Ball tool
Paintbrush

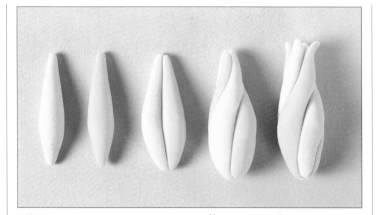

1 Colour half the paste grey and half pink. Roll out some grey paste and cut out the base of the vase using a 5cm (2 inch) cutter. Emboss the base (see page 7) if you wish.

2 Roll two pink and two grey pieces of paste into 7.5cm (3 inch) long teardrop shapes and fix them together as illustrated. Twist the assembled pieces together to produce a spiral effect.

3 Open out the top section with a ball tool and create a 3.5cm (1½ inch) deep neck on the vase. Flatten the tip of each section of paste between finger and thumb and curl downwards and outwards.

4 Flatten a ball of pink paste into a 1cm (½ inch) diameter disc and fix in the centre of the round base with glue. Fix the base of the vase on to this and allow to dry.

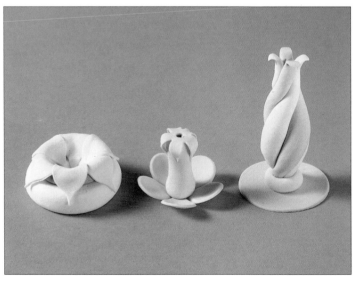

Wheelbarrow

By making a few simple additions to the basic design, this cake top can be used for celebrations such as retirement, Father's Day, or a lady's birthday.

Materials

90g (3oz) mexican paste/pastillage (see page 42)
Black, dark brown and egg yellow food colourings
Royal icing (see page 42)
Edible glue
Caster (superfine) sugar and brown dusting powder (petal dust/blossom tint) or demerara sugar

For a man's cake

45g (1½oz) mexican paste/pastillage (see page 42)
Christmas green, liquorice black, dark brown and orange food colourings
Green dusting powder (petal dust/blossom tint)

For a lady's cake

45g (1½oz) mexican paste/pastillage (see page 42)
Claret, egg yellow, Christmas green and dark brown food colourings

Equipment

10cm (4 inch) round cutter or thin cake board
Dresden tool
Craft knife or scalpel
Greaseproof paper (parchment) piping bag
No. 1 piping tube (tip)
Smallest centre from Garrett frill cutter

For a man's cake

2.5cm (1 inch) blossom cutter
Cocktail stick (toothpick)

For a lady's cake

Fine scissors
Small calyx cutter

Base

1 To create the paving effect, colour 45g (1½oz) paste grey using a small amount of black colour and roll out until 5mm (¼ inch) thick. Use a cutter to cut out a 10cm (4 inch) disc or place the paste over the cake board and trim away excess round the edge.

2 Mark parallel grooves, about 1cm (½ inch) apart, across the disc using the veiner end of a dresden tool. Mark a second set of shorter parallel lines at right angles to and in between the first set, about 2.5cm (1 inch) apart to create the effect of paving slabs.

Wheelbarrow

3 Colour 45g (1½oz) paste with equal quantities of dark brown and egg yellow food colourings. Roll out a thin sheet and mark the surface with short irregular lines with the veiner end of the dresden tool to give the effect of wood grain.

4 Cut out the sections needed for the wheelbarrow using templates made from the outlines on page 46. Allow to dry for 24 hours.

5. Assemble the sections of the barrow, sticking them together with royal icing coloured to match the paste sections. Using a paper piping bag fitted with a no. 1 tube, pipe the icing along the edges of the sections before pushing them firmly together. Allow to dry.

6. Roll out another piece of brown paste to 2.5mm (⅛ inch) thick and cut out the wheel for the barrow using the smallest centre of the Garrett frill cutter.

7. Cut two thin pieces of paste 3cm (1¼ inches) in length and allow to dry. Sandwich the wheel between the two strips and fix to the underside of the barrow.

8. Roll a long cylinder of brown paste about 2.5mm (⅛ inch) in diameter. Flatten gently with a rolling pin, leaving about 2.5cm (1 inch) at one end unflattened. Cut to a length of

7.5cm (3 inches). Repeat for the second handle. Allow to dry, then attach to the barrow.

9. For the legs of the barrow, roll a 3.5cm (1½ inch) cylinder of paste tapered at each end. Cut in half and allow to dry. Fix to the barrow.

10. Place 2 teaspoons caster sugar in a small bowl, add ½ teaspoon brown dusting powder and stir until the sugar turns brown. (Alternatively, use demerara sugar.) Spoon some of this 'soil' into the barrow and put a small amount on the 'paving'. Fix the barrow to the 'paving'.

Optional extras

11. For a man's cake, add a garden spade and some vegetables to the ornament. For carrots, form small orange cones and roll them with a cocktail stick until tapered at one end. Add small peices of green paste to the blunt ends for carrot tops. Mark lines across the carrots in places for a realistic effect.

12. For a cauliflower, roll a 5mm (¼ inch) ball of white paste and prick half the surface of the ball with a pin. Using a 2.5cm (1 inch) blossom cutter, cut out a blossom shape from a thin sheet of green paste. Frill each petal by rolling with a cocktail stick. Place the cauliflower head in the centre of the petals and gather them up around it. Once dry, dust with green dusting powder.

13. For a marrow, roll some pale green paste into a 2.5cm (1 inch) cylinder, slightly narrower in the centre. Allow to dry, then dust with stripes of dark green powder.

14. To make a garden shovel, cut out a rectangle of grey paste measuring 1.5 x 2.5cm (¾ x 1 inch). Roll a cocktail stick

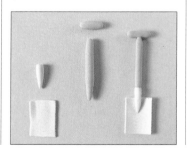

from long side to long side to slightly curve the paste for the shovel head. Roll a 1.5cm (¾ inch) cone of grey paste and hollow out the blunt end. Fix the pointed end on to the shovel head. Roll out a 3cm (1¼ inch) cylinder of brown paste, and taper it at one end. Allow to dry. Fix the tapered end into the opening on the shaft of the shovel head. Roll a 1.5cm (¾ inch) cylinder of brown paste to form the handle, and attach when dry.

▷15▷ For a lady's cake, add a hat, gloves and daffodils. To make a hat, cut a disc of dark pink paste using the small centre from the Garrett frill cutter. Frill the edge with a cocktail stick and allow to dry. Flatten a small ball of paste between finger and thumb and fix to the centre of the disc. Roll a 5cm (2 inch) long strip of paste and fix it around the base of the crown of the hat. Overlap the strip where it joins to form tails. Snip a 'V' in the end of each tail. Make a small bow (see page 30).

▷16▷ Roll out a thin piece of paste and cut out gloves using a template made from the pattern on page 46.

▷17▷ For daffodils, roll a thin length of green paste and cut three strips for the stems. Cut out four small calyxes from pale egg yellow paste. Cut one calyx into individual sepals, and add one sepal to each of the other calyxes to give six petals

for each daffodil. Roll a small white or yellow cone, place a cocktail stick in the pointed end and roll to open and thin out the throat. Fix on to the petals and attach the flower to the stem.

Wishing Well

This Wishing Well is ideal for birthdays, get well, retirement, even Valentine's Day – in fact for whenever you want to send good wishes to someone.

Materials

200g (6½ oz) mexican paste/pastillage (see page 42)
Christmas red, Christmas green, dark brown, egg yellow and liquorice black food colourings
30g (1oz) sugarpaste (ready-to-roll icing)
Brown dusting powder (petal dust/blossom tint)
Royal icing (see page 42)

Equipment

Craft knife or scalpel
Tea strainer (optional)
Cardboard roll from centre of absorbent kitchen paper
Basketweave rolling pin
5.5cm (2¼ inch) and 4cm (1½ inch) round cutters
Dresden tool
Fine paintbrush
Small heart or blossom plunger cutter
Greaseproof paper (parchment) piping bags
Nos. 0 and 1 piping tubes (tips)
No. ST50 PME leaf tube (tip)

Base

1 Roll out a sheet of pale cream coloured paste and cut out a plaque using a template made from the outline on page 46.

2 Roll 22g (¾oz) of the sugarpaste into a sausage shape, and fix it around the top left edge of the plaque, smoothing it into position to give a neat join where it meets the plaque.

3 Colour 30g (1oz) mexican paste/pastillage Christmas green. Roll out and fix it on to the plaque, covering the sausage of sugarpaste and leaving enough of the plaque exposed to write an inscription, if you wish. Trim away excess. Texture the green paste if you wish by pressing a tea strainer over it.

Well

4 Cover one end of the cardboard roll with a 5cm (2 inch) deep piece of greaseproof paper.

5 Colour 60g (2oz) paste using equal quantities of Christmas red and dark brown to produce a red brick tone. Roll

out a sheet 2.5mm (⅛ inch) thick and roll over once with the basketweave pin. Cut a strip measuring 20 x 4cm (8 x 1½ inches). Wrap the paste around the cardboard roll, over the paper, and place a second piece of paper over the paste. Secure with tape or a paper clip. Allow to dry, then remove from the roll.

6 Roll a second rectangle of brick red paste, texture as before and fit it inside the first piece. Allow to dry.

7 Roll out 7g (¼oz) grey paste and cut out a 5.5cm (2¼ inch) round. Remove the centre using a 4cm (1½ inch) cutter. Score the paste with a dresden tool and allow to dry. Paint the grooves black and dust the rest with brown.

8 From 7g (¼oz) black paste cut a disc the same diameter as the cardboard roll. Attach to the plaque and fix the well on top. Fix the grey ring on top of the well 'wall'.

Roof

9 Cut two rectangles of brick red paste each measuring 4 x 5cm (1½ x 2 inches). Allow to dry.

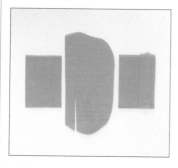

10 Roll out a sheet of brick red paste and score with parallel lines at 5mm (¼ inch) intervals. Cut into strips measuring 5 x 1cm (2 x ½ inch), cutting at right-angles to the scored lines. Attach to the previously cut rectangles so that they overlap and each is staggered to give the effect of tiles. Keep adding strips until only a thin piece at the top of each rectangle is exposed.

11 Colour 45g (1½oz) mexican paste/pastillage a pale shade of dark brown. Roll out to 2.5mm (⅛ inch) thick and score the paste using the dresden tool to give a wood grain effect (see page 10). Cut two triangles using a template made from the outline on page 46.

Using a plunger cutter, cut out the centre of each triangle. Allow to dry.

12 Cut a strip of the brown paste measuring 6 x 1 x 0.5cm (2½ x ½ x ¼ inch), and cut a 4.5cm (1¾ inch) split in one end. Open the ends and attach to the triangle as illustrated, using royal icing coloured to match the paste in a bag fitted with a no. 1 tube. Repeat with a second strip. Allow to dry. Attach the tiled roof sections to the triangular end pieces.

13 Roll a 3.5cm (1¼ inch) long cylinder of brown paste. Allow to dry, then pipe yellow lines around it using royal icing in a greaseproof paper piping bag fitted with a no. 1 piping tube to represent the rope. Fix between the uprights.

14 Attach the roof and upright sections to the base of the well. Cut a 5 x 1cm (2 x ½ inch) strip of brick red paste and score. Attach to the top of the well roof. Lightly dust the roof sections with brown dusting powder.

Bucket

15 Mould a cone from the remaining sugarpaste and trim off each end to give a shape 2.5cm (1 inch) tall with a diameter of 2cm (¾ inch) at one end and 2.5cm (1 inch) at the other. Allow to dry.

16 Roll out 15g (½oz) dark brown paste and score with the veiner end of the dresden tool to produce a wood grain effect (see page 10). Cut out a 2cm (¾ inch) diameter disc for the bucket base and a strip measuring 2.5 x 7cm (1 x 2¾ inches). Dust the previously made bucket mould with cornflour. Place the disc on the small end and fix the strip around the sides. Allow to dry, then remove from the mould and dust with brown dusting powder. Fix in position, next to the well.

17 Using yellow royal icing and a no. 1 piping tube, pipe the rope dangling from the well spindle, and the rope handle on the bucket.

18 With green royal icing and a no. 0 piping tube, pipe grass and ivy stems up the side of the well and on to the roof. Using a no. ST50 PME leaf tube, pipe on ivy leaves.

Tip

If you haven't got the right PME leaf tube (tip), you can pipe the leaves from a bag with a 'V' shape cut in the tip.

Mouse Valentine Plaque

Ideally suited to a Valentine's cake, this design could equally well be used on a cake made to celebrate a birthday or engagement.

Materials

125g (4oz) mexican paste/pastillage (see page 42)
Mulberry, Christmas green, chestnut and liquorice black food colourings
Edible glue
Brown and pink dusting powders (petal dust/blossom tint)
White fat (shortening)

Equipment

10cm (4 inch) heart cutter
Rose embosser
Fine paintbrush
Dresden tool
Ball tool
Craft knife or scalpel
Plunger blossom cutter

Plaque

1 Roll out some mexican paste/pastillage and cut out a heart-shaped plaque (see page 7). Emboss as required and leave to dry. Paint or dust the embossed pattern.

Mouse

2 Make a template from the mouse illustration on page 46, and use to cut a thin plaque from paste.

3 To make the mouse's feet, roll a small oval of pale chestnut paste for the left and a long cone for the right foot. Fix the left foot in position on the mouse plaque with edible glue and mark the toes using the sharp end of the dresden tool. Fix the right foot so that it overlaps the left.

4 The mouse's left foreleg is made by rolling a small oval and fixing in position. Flatten out the left side of this piece.

5 For the body, first roll a cylinder measuring 4 x 2cm (1½ x ¾ inch). Place your finger on the piece just off-centre, and gently roll back and forth to produce a kidney shape. Fix on to the plaque so that it slightly overlaps the foreleg. Smooth out to the edge of the mouse plaque.

6 Attach a thin piece of white paste for the chest and stomach. Roll an oval of chestnut paste 2cm (¾ inch) long and fix it in place to form the right foreleg.

7 The right hind leg is made by flattening a ball of chestnut paste 1cm (½ inch)

in diameter to form a 2cm (¾ inch) disc with a plump centre.

8 For the ears, form a small ball of paste 5mm (¼ inch) in diameter. Cut in half to make the two ears and place one under a sheet of plastic food wrap until later. Roll the other piece into a ball and cup with the ball tool. Place this in position on the plaque, cup down, to form the left ear.

9 Make the mouse's head from a cone of paste measuring 2.5 x 2cm (1 x ¾ inch) at the base. Place in position and smooth out until it reaches the edge of the plaque and overlaps the mouse's left ear and shoulder slightly. With a craft knife or scalpel, mark in the mouth. Use a ball tool to make indentations for the eye and nose.

10 Roll the second ear piece into a ball. Take a small piece of pale mulberry-coloured paste and place it on top of the ear piece, attaching it by pressing it in with the ball tool. This creates a cupped ear with a pink lining. Attach to the head. Dust the mouse with brown dusting powder.

11 To make an eye, place a small piece of white paste in the eye socket and secure with the ball tool. Add a tiny ball of black paste. Fix a ball of black paste in the nose depression and mark the nostrils. Give a shine to the nose and a twinkle in the eye by brushing with white fat, which is soft enough to brush without melting. Brush a little pink dust over the mouse's cheek.

12 The flowers can be made using a blossom plunger cutter. The mouse's tail is a thin tapered sausage of pale chestnut paste. Fix the mouse on to the heart with edible glue.

Tip

A fur effect can be created by making short cuts over the body while still soft, using a craft knife or scalpel.

Bunny Valentine Plaque

This cute little bunny with his deep red heart is perfect for sending love on Valentine's Day.

Materials

125g (4oz) mexican paste/
pastillage (see page 42)
Cyclamen and brown dusting
powders (petal dust/blossom
tint)
Ruby, chestnut, mulberry, egg
yellow and liquorice food colourings
Edible glue

Equipment

10cm (4 inch) heart cutter
Cocktail stick (toothpick)
No. 8 or no. 10 paintbrush
Ball tool
Craft knife or scalpel

Plaque

1 Roll out 45g (1½oz) mexican paste/pastillage and cut out a heart shape. Frill the edges with a cocktail stick and leave to dry. Dust the edges with cyclamen dusting powder.

Heart

2 Roll 30g (1oz) ruby red paste into a ball, then flatten it to a disc that is thinner at the edge than in the middle.

3 Make a template from the outline on page 46, and use to cut out a heart shape. Smooth the edges, and dry.

Rabbit

4 Colour 30g (1oz) paste pale chestnut. To make the rabbit's front paws, cut a small ball of chestnut paste in half and roll each half into a cone. Cup each cone by dragging a ball tool from the base to the tip. Attach the pointed end of each cone to the back of the heart with edible glue, and fold the opposite end over the top of the heart. Mark the toes with a craft knife or scalpel.

5 For the back paws, roll a 3cm (1¼ inch) cylinder of chestnut paste and thin it in the middle. Mark toes in each end

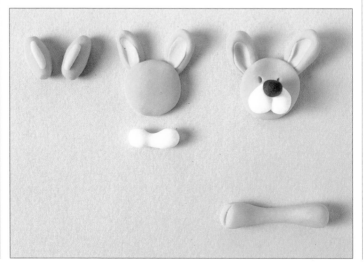

with a craft knife. Attach to the heart so it overlaps the centre of the cylinder, creating the impression of separate feet.

6 For the ears, roll a 1cm (½ inch) oval of chestnut paste and a smaller oval of pale mulberry-coloured paste. Press the mulberry oval on to the chestnut oval with a ball tool to create a cupped ear. Repeat to make the second ear.

7 To make the head, flatten a ball of chestnut paste into a 2cm (¾ inch) diameter disc. Attach the ears to the back. Roll a 1cm (½ inch) cylinder of white paste. Thin the middle section by rolling back and forth with your finger to form a dumb-bell shape, then fold the two ends down until they meet. Attach to the face of the rabbit to form the mouth section.

8 Dust the rabbit with brown dusting powder, then make the eyes and nose. With a ball tool, make impressions in the rabbit's face for the eye sockets and a nose. Make two small balls of black paste and fix them into the eye sockets. Place a ball of black paste into the nose depression and mark nostrils.

9 Cut a small disc of chestnut/egg yellow paste, about 8mm (⅓ inch) in diameter. (You could use the base of a piping tube to do this.) Make a series of short cuts around the edge with a craft knife and soften the edge with a ball tool. Fix to the head for the rabbit's 'hair'. Attach the head and heart to the plaque.

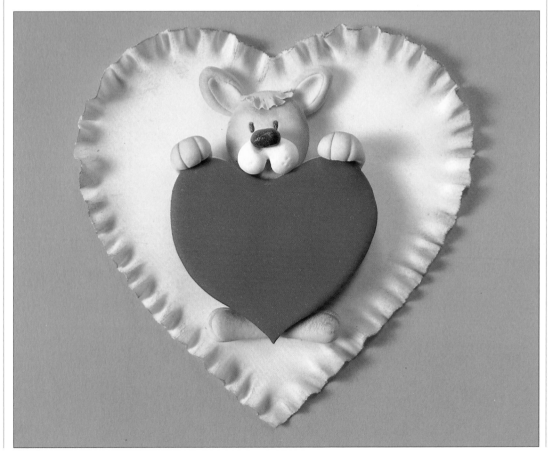

Blackberry Casket

As well as looking attractive in itself, this casket has the added appeal that you can hide something inside it – a favourite chocolate, a sugar flower, perhaps a ring. . .

Materials

45g (1½oz) claret-coloured mexican paste/pastillage (see page 42)
60g (2oz) pale green mexican paste/pastillage (see page 42)
Green and brown dusting powders (petal dust/blossom tint)
Royal icing (see page 42)
15g (½oz) dark green mexican paste/pastillage (see page 42)
30g (1oz) blackberry-coloured mexican paste/pastillage (see page 42)
White fat (shortening)
Edible glue

Equipment

Garrett frill or large biscuit cutter
Embosser or button
25cm (10 inch) length of lace
Soft paintbrush (no. 10)
Cardboard roll from centre of absorbent kitchen paper
6cm (2½ inch) scone cutter
Greaseproof paper (parchment) piping bag
Nos. 0, 1 and 2 piping tubes (tips)
Leaf cutter, such as rose leaf
Ball tool
Dresden tool or leaf veiner
Cocktail stick (toothpick)
Small calyx cutter

Base

1 Roll out the claret-coloured paste and cut out a plaque using the Garrett frill or large biscuit cutter. Emboss as required (see page 7).

Casket

2 Cut a strip of pale green paste measuring 4.5 x 22cm (1¾ x 8½ inches), and place the lace lengthways down the middle. Roll over gently with a rolling pin to secure.

3 Cover the paste either side of the lace with strips of greaseproof paper, then dust over the lace using a soft brush and green powder. Remove the paper and the lace. Fix the paste around the cardboard roll and allow to dry.

Casket lid and base

4 Cut the lid and base of the casket using a 6cm (2½ inch) scone cutter. Allow to dry.

5 Remove the casket from the cardboard roll and attach the base using royal icing in a greaseproof paper piping bag fitted with a no. 2 tube.

6 Dust the top of the casket with icing sugar and rest the lid in place. Remove the lid and there will be a circular mark on the underneath. Roll a cylinder of mexican paste/pastillage and attach as a ring within this mark. This will stop the lid sliding off the casket.

Leaves

7 Roll out the dark green paste and cut out five leaves. Soften the edges with a ball tool, and vein the leaves. Curl the leaves slightly and allow to dry.

Blackberries

8 Roll a lot of small balls from the blackberry-coloured paste, and allow to dry. Form two cones of blackberry paste 1cm (½ inch) long.

10 Finish the blackberries by adding a small calyx cut from dark green paste to each fruit. Allow to dry.

11 Attach the leaves and blackberries to the lid of the casket. Pipe the pattern illustrated using the no. 0 tube with green royal icing and a no. 1 tube with blackberry-coloured icing.

Tip

An alternative casket can be made using six after-dinner mints. Use one mint for the base and four to form the sides, fixing them together by melting the edges with a hot teaspoon. The sixth mint forms the lid. This quick and easy casket can be filled with truffles and decorated with sugar flowers.

9 Grease the tip of a cocktail stick with a little white fat and insert it into one of the cones. Coat the cone with glue and cover with small balls of paste. When completely covered, remove from the stick and leave to dry. Repeat for the remaining cone.

22

The Night Before Christmas

Santa has a small snack before setting off to deliver presents! This modelled cake top is sure to delight everyone, especially the children.

Materials

250g (8oz) marzipan (almond paste)
Dark brown, Christmas red, chestnut, blueberry, Christmas green and liquorice food colourings

Equipment

10cm (4 inch) thin round cake board
Dresden tool
Ball tool
No. 1 or no. 2 paintbrush
Cocktail stick (toothpick)

Board

1 Colour 15g (½oz) marzipan dark brown, roll out and use to cover the board.

2 With the veiner (sharp) end of the dresden tool, make a series of short strokes over the entire surface of the marzipan. This will create a wood grain effect.

3 Using a ruler as a guide, draw parallel lines across the surface of the marzipan with the veiner end of the dresden tool, applying greater pressure than when creating the wood grain effect in step 2, to make the floorboards.

Chair

4 Cut a rectangular block of green marzipan measuring 4.5 x 4 x 1cm (1¾ x 1½ x ½ inch), and score the sides with the broad end of the dresden tool. Place in the centre of the covered board.

5 Cut another block of marzipan measuring 4.5 x 4 x 1.5cm (1¾ x 1½ x ⅝ inch), and place this on top of the first to form the base of the chair.

6 Roll two cylinders of marzipan 4cm (1½ inches) long and 5mm (¼ inch) in diameter, and place one on top of each short side of the chair.

7 Roll two cylinders of marzipan 4cm (1½ inches) long and 1.5cm (⅝ inch) in diameter, and place one on top of each of the cylinders made in step 6. To complete the arms of the chair, indent one end of each with the small end of a ball tool, and fix a ball of green paste in this indent.

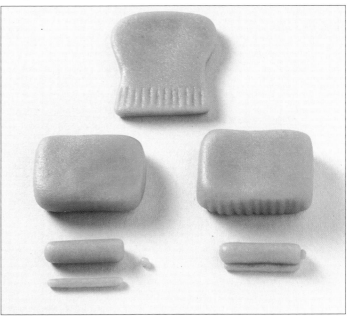

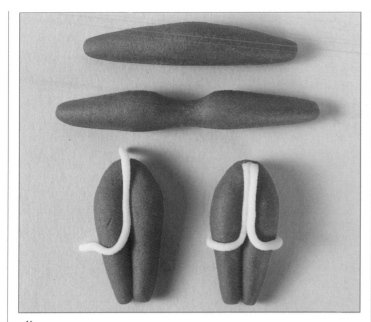

8 ▷ Make the back of the chair by rolling a 1cm (½ inch) thick sheet of marzipan and cutting out a section using a template made from the outline on page 47. Round off the cut edges. Score the base with the broad end of the dresden tool, and fix in position.

Tip

Marzipan is often soft enough to stick together unaided, but use a little water or edible glue if necessary.

Santa

9 ▷ Roll a 15cm (6 inch) cylinder of red marzipan so that the centre measures 2cm (¾ inch) in diameter and tapers off at each end to 1cm (½ inch). Place your forefinger on the centre of the cylinder and roll back and forth to thin the middle down to 1cm (½ inch). Fold the cylinder in half and place in the chair with the fold upright and the tapered ends bending over the front of the chair.

10 ▷ Roll a 7.5cm (3 inch) thin cylinder of natural coloured marzipan, and run this down the centre of the body from top to bottom for 5cm (2 inches), then turn across and round the right leg. Repeat with a second length of marzipan but this time fold across the left leg. This creates the fur edging to the cloak.

11 ▷ Roll two cylinders of marzipan 5cm (2 inches) long and 1.5cm (⅝ inch) in diameter, and fold the middle of each at a right angle. Fix in position to form the arms. Create a socket in the end of each arm using a ball tool.

12 ▷ Roll a 2.5 cm (1 inch) diameter ball of pale chestnut paste for the head. For the beard, mould a triangle of natural marzipan and pull out two corners. Score with the dresden tool and fix on to the head with the pulled corners running up the sides of the face. Roll a tapered cylinder of natural marzipan for the moustache and fix into position.

13 Roll two tiny balls of chestnut marzipan and one larger ball to form the nostrils and the nose. Mark the eye sockets using the ball tool and complete by adding a small piece of natural and black marzipan to each socket.

14 Cut a length of natural marzipan and score with the dresden tool. Fix around the sides and back of the head for the hair. If you do not wish your Santa to be bald, then press out a 2.5cm (1 inch) disc of natural marzipan and score with the dresden tool to give the impression of hair and a centre parting. Fix to the top of the head.

15 Roll two small cones of natural marzipan for the eyebrows.

16 Roll a small cone of chestnut paste for one hand, flatten between finger and thumb and cut to form the thumb and four fingers. Roll each between finger and thumb to neaten. Repeat for a second hand, then fix each into the sockets in the ends of the arms.

17 For the mug, roll a 1cm (½ inch) cylinder of natural marzipan, flatten one end and make a slight depression in the other end with the ball tool. Flatten a small disk of brown paste and place in the depression. Roll a thin piece of marzipan to form the handle and bend the fingers round to hold the mug.

27

18 Roll a 5mm (¼ inch) ball of pale brown paste, flatten slightly and pinch the edge. Mark round the edge with the veining end of the dresden tool. Cut a section out and paint the filling of the mince pie with a fine brush and a little dark brown food colouring. Bend the fingers to hold the mince pie.

19 Roll a cylinder of black paste measuring 2.5cm (1 inch) long by 1cm (½ inch) in diameter. Flatten one end between finger and thumb, and fold the other end at a right angle to form the left boot. Fix in position, then repeat for the right boot.

20 Roll thin sausages of natural marzipan and fix around the wrists and the top of the boots to neaten the joins.

Decorations

21 Make the calendar by cutting a small square block of natural marzipan. Paint on the figure 24 with a no. 1 or no. 2 brush.

22 Using small pieces of blue marzipan, form a rectangular and a square block and mark opposite sides with the dresden tool to create the impression of paper-wrapped parcels. Roll a 2.5cm (1 inch) cylinder of yellow paste. Place a cocktail stick within 5mm (¼ inch) of the end and roll back and forth. Repeat at the other end. Indent the ends to complete the cracker.

23 For instructions for making the wreath decorations on the side of the cake, see page 43.

Variation

An ornament for Father's Day or Grandpa's birthday can be made in much the same way as Santa, with the following variations:

1 The figure is dressed in pyjamas; press a thin cylinder of blue paste on to the jacket to form the breast pocket. Place a 'V'-shaped piece of chestnut paste on the top half of the body with a thin strip of pale blue, cut to shape, around the edge to give the impression of an open-necked pyjama jacket.

2 In one hand the figure holds an envelope; in the other a card. The envelope is made from a square of thin white paste which has had three of the corners folded into the centre, while the card is a square folded in half with a painted design on one side.

3 The slippers are made from paste coloured with equal quantities of dark brown and egg yellow. Roll a short cylinder for each slipper and flatten slightly where it will be joined to the end of the leg. The bears' faces are made in the same way as for the Child's Teddy Card (see page 32), as are the parcels, tags and bows. Thin dark blue strips of paste are fixed to the pale blue parcel to give the effect of stripes.

4 For the envelopes on the board, cut rectangles of paste, paint thin black lines on some and score the others with the veining end of the dresden tool.

5 Make the bottle from a short cylinder tapered at one end. Make fine cuts along one edge of a thin strip of paste and then roll the paste up from short side to short side to make the tassle on the top of the bottle.

Tip

The heads of the figures can be made from a round truffle covered with chestnut marzipan. This gives a nice surprise to whoever bites the head off (and, let's face it, somebody always does!).

Child's Teddy Card

The bears are working feverishly to put the final touches to somebody's special card, making this ornament a delight for any child between the ages of 2 and 92!

Materials

315g (10oz) mexican paste/pastillage (see page 42)
Claret, egg yellow, dark brown, blueberry and liquorice food colourings
Edible glue
Royal icing (see page 42)

Equipment

JEM plain card cutter (11 x 7.5cm/4½ x 3 inches)
Dresden tool
7cm (2¾ inch) oval cutter
Greaseproof paper (parchment) piping bag
No. 2 piping tube (tip)
Soft paintbrush (no. 2 or 3)
Craft knife or scalpel
Cocktail stick (toothpick)
Ball tool

'Envelope' plaque

1 Roll out 90g (3oz) claret mexican paste/pastillage until 2.5mm (⅛ inch) thick. Cut out a section using the card cutter. Use the veining end of the dresden tool to mark two grooves running from the corners of one long side to the centre of the opposite long side. Cut another thin sheet of claret paste, then trim to a triangular shape for the flap of the envelope. Fix into position on top of the first envelope piece, and allow to dry.

Card

2 Roll out some white paste and cut out two card sections. Remove the centre from one using the oval cutter. Allow to dry.

3 Cut a thin strip of claret paste measuring 18cm x 9.5mm (7 x ⅜ inch), and cut a 'V' in each end. Attach the centre of the strip to the top right of the oval window. Twist each half round the window and moisten the ends to fix in place. Cut a 6 x 1.5cm (2½ x ¾ inch) strip and fold each end into the

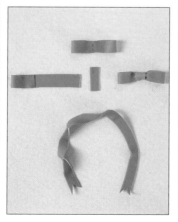

centre. Squeeze the centre together using the dresden tool, and wrap a thin piece of paste round the centre to complete the bow. Attach to the card front.

4 Assemble the sections of the card on the 'envelope' plaque using royal icing in a greaseproof paper piping bag fitted with a no. 2 piping tube. Neaten the joins and remove excess icing using a slightly dampened soft paintbrush.

Teddy bears

5 Colour 125g (4oz) paste using equal quantities of egg yellow and dark brown. Divide in two and set one piece aside. Cut the first piece in two with one section slightly larger than the other.

6 Divide the larger piece in two and roll one half into a pear shape. Press the base of the pear on either side with the finger and thumb and make slight depressions for the legs to fit into. Divide the other piece in two, and roll each into a long cone. Thin the middle of each cone slightly and form a ball at the narrow end. Slightly flatten the ball and turn up to make a foot. Mark the toes with a craft

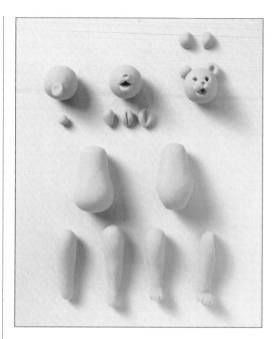

knife. Cut the top of each leg at an angle and fix the cut surface into the depression on the body to produce a seated bear.

▷7◁ Make another claret bow, as above (step 3), but cut the tails from a 4cm (1½ inch) length of paste. Fix into position on the bear.

▷8◁ Cut the other piece of paste in half. Form the arms in the same way as the legs but after flattening the paw cut a thumb and fingers. Twist each thumb and finger to neaten the cut surfaces. Attach the arms and arrange the paws so they are holding the bow, with little fingers extended.

▷9◁ Roll a 1cm (½ inch) ball of white paste and flatten into a 2.5mm (⅛ inch) disc. Use the dresden tool to shape a tri-angular depression in the disc to form the opening of the collar. Roll a tiny piece of black paste into a dumb-bell shape using a cocktail stick, and pinch each end to a point. Use the craft knife to mark the centre of the bow and attach to the collar. Fix in position on the bear.

▷10◁ Trim a small piece off the remaining piece of paste to use later for the nose and ears, and roll the rest into a ball for the head. Mark two eye sockets with the ball tool and complete the eyes with small pieces of white and black paste.

▷11◁ Take a small ball of bear-coloured paste, cup with the ball tool and fix on to the lower half of the face to form the lower jaw. Take a slightly larger piece of paste, roll into a short, fat cone and split halfway through the length. Open out and smooth the cut surface. Fix the wider end on to the face so it overlaps the lower jaw. Mark a depression for the nose. Place a small triangle of black paste in the depression and mark in nostrils with the veining end of the dresden tool. A tiny ball of claret paste secured with the dresden tool makes the tongue.

▷12◁ Cut a 9.5mm (⅜ inch) ball of bear-coloured paste in half and roll each half back into a ball. Fix to the top of the head for the ears and push in and down with the ball tool to cup the ear and secure in position.

▷13◁ Repeat steps 5–12, above, to make a second bear in the same way, but as this bear is to stand, allow the legs to dry thoroughly before fixing the body in position.

Parcel

14 Add equal quantities of blueberry and claret food colourings to 30g (1oz) paste. Pinch off a small piece of paste and form the remainder into a rectangular block for the present. Mark the square ends to give the impression of a paper-wrapped parcel.

15 Cut a small tag from white paste. Cut three thin strips of claret paste to make the bow. Fold the ends of each over towards the middle but leave a small gap. Fix the strips on top of each other on the par-

cel. Finally, cut a fourth, shorter strip and form into a circle. Fix this into the centre of the bow.

Can and brush

16 Roll a tiny cone of bear-coloured paste for the tip of the brush and make a small indent in the blunt end. Roll a longer cone from claret paste. Roll the blunt end to a point and fix into the brush tip.

17 Roll a 2cm (¾ inch) long cylinder of 1cm (½ inch) diameter from white paste. With the small piece of blueberry/ claret paste reserved when making the parcel, make a disc for the top of the cylinder. Roll a strip of white paste slightly deeper than the cylinder and long enough to wrap around to complete the paint can. Roll tiny cones of paste to form drips of paint

18 With a fine brush, paint the start of an inscription on the inside of the card.

19 For instructions for completing the side decorations on the cake, see page 44.

Countryside Card

Suitable for a retirement, new home or birthday, this card uses appliqué and découpage to whisk you away from the hubbub of everyday life.

Materials

185g (6oz) mexican paste/pastillage (see page 42)
Egg yellow, dark brown, chestnut, blueberry, Christmas green and liquorice food colourings
Brown and green dusting powders (petal dust/blossom tint)
Royal icing (see page 42)

Equipment

JEM plain card cutter (11 x 7.5cm/4½ x 3 inches)
Craft knife or scalpel
Soft paintbrushes (nos. 2 and 4)
Large soft paintbrush (no. 8 or 10)
Greaseproof paper (parchment) piping bag
No. 1, no. ST50 and no. 2 piping tubes (tips)
Ball tool
Dresden tool

Card

1 Colour 45g (1½oz) paste pale blue with blueberry food colouring, and roll out to a thin sheet. Cut out a section for the back of the card with the card cutter. Make a template from the outline on page 47 and use to trim the top right corner to shape. Allow to dry.

2 Colour 45g (1½oz) paste dark brown and roll out to a thin sheet. Cut out a section with the card cutter, and cut to shape using a template made from the outline on page 47. Allow to dry. Paint fine lines of dark brown on the cut-out piece and dust with brown dusting powder to give the effect of bark. Pipe leaves using green royal icing with a no. ST50 piping tube. When dry, dust with green dusting powder.

Hedges and hill

3 Using templates made from the outlines on page 47, cut the hedge sections and far hill from 15g (½oz) pale Christmas green paste. Turn the hill section over and run the ball tool just inside the top edge to curve slightly. Allow to dry. Dust the hill from the base upwards

with green dusting powder. Pipe green royal icing over the hedge sections and stipple with a no. 4 brush. Allow to dry, then dust with brown and green.

4 Cut the bank section from 15g (½oz) darker Christmas green paste and curve the top edge as above. Allow to dry. Dust from the base upwards with green.

Cottage and gate

5 Cut out the cottage from 15g (½oz) white paste. Allow to dry. Paint windows and a door with a fine paintbrush and liquorice black and brown food colourings. Colour some royal icing using equal quantities of egg yellow and dark brown and pipe on to the roof using a no. 1 piping tube. Texture with a fine paintbrush.

6 Roll out 15g (½oz) paste coloured with equal quantities of egg yellow and dark brown food colouring and give it a wood grain effect by texturing with the veining end of the dresden tool. Cut two strips of paste measuring 3cm x 2.5mm (1¼ x ⅛ inch) for the gate bars, one strip measuring 6cm x 5mm (2½ x ¼ inch) for the signpost, and a strip measuring 2.5cm x 5mm (1 x ¼ inch) for the sign. Allow to dry. Dust lightly with brown.

7 Roll 15g (½oz) chestnut paste and fix to the back of the card to form the path.

Assembly

8 Assemble the sections using royal icing in a greaseproof paper piping bag fitted with a no. 2 tube and, finally, fix the two halves of the card together. Neaten the joins with a dampened fine brush.

Rocking Crib

This delicate crib is a simple but effective design suitable for a Christening. The items shown around the crib are only a few ideas, there are many more that could be used.

Materials

125g (4oz) mexican paste/pastillage (see page 42)
Egg yellow, blueberry, Christmas green, claret, liquorice and chestnut food colourings
Royal icing (see page 42)
Edible glue

Equipment

11cm (4½ inch) oval plaque cutter
Dresden tool
4cm (1½ inch) and 2.5cm (1 inch) heart cutters
5cm (2 inch) and 4cm (1½ inch) round cutters
Greaseproof paper (parchment) piping bag
No. 1 piping tube (tip)
Heart plunger cutter
Cocktail stick (toothpick)
Ball tool
Fine paintbrush

Variations

The head and tail boards of the crib can be decorated with a variety of plunger cutter pieces or piped work, or even a painted scene. The coloured building blocks could be used to spell out the child's name or the date of the Christening.

Base

1 Roll out 45g (1½oz) pale egg yellow paste and cut out an 11cm (4½ inch) oval plaque. Emboss the edge with a dresden tool, then allow to dry.

Crib

2 Roll out 45g (1½oz) pale blueberry paste and cut one 4cm (1½ inch) and one 2.5cm (1 inch) heart. Also cut out a disc with a 5cm (2 inch) round cutter and a 4.5 x 4cm (1¾ x 1½ inch) rectangle. Dry the rectangle of paste over a rolling pin so that the shorter sides are curved. Remove the centre from the disc with a 4cm (1½ inch) round cutter, and cut two sections for the rockers. Allow to dry.

3 Assemble the sections and pipe edging around the edges of the crib using some blue royal icing in a greaseproof paper piping bag fitted with a no. 1 tube.

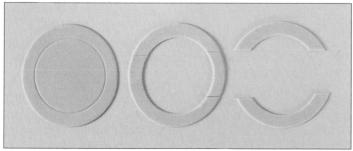

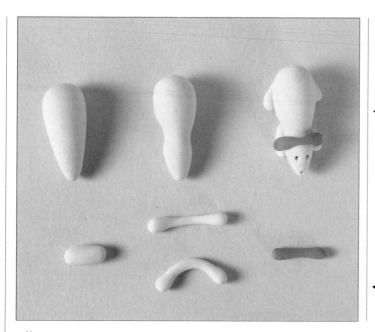

8 Mould the dog from 15g (½ oz) chestnut paste. Roll a short cone, roll just in from the narrow end with a cocktail stick to form the head and body in one go. Roll a thin cylinder for the tail. Roll a cylinder and taper in the middle for the ears. Repeat for the legs. Complete by marking the eyes and nose with a cocktail stick.

9 For instructions for making the side cake decorations, see page 45.

4 Roll out some white paste and cut out a heart with a plunger cutter. Attach to the end of the crib with edible glue.

5 Mould a pillow from 7g (¼ oz) white paste and place in the crib. Cut a 4cm (1½ inch) square of white paste for the blanket and frill the edges with a cocktail stick.

Toys

6 Roll some pale claret and Christmas green/blueberry paste into sheets 5mm (¼ inch) thick and cut into blocks.

7 Mould the elephant from 15g (½ oz) grey paste. Roll a tapered cone for the head, with two small cupped balls for the ears and a ball for the body. The legs are four small balls. Complete by painting or piping on eyes.

Convertible Car

Based on a mould for an egg, this sporty number can be used to top a wedding cake, bon voyage cake, birthday cake, or to say congratulations on passing your driving test.

Materials

250g (8oz) mexican paste/pastillage (see page 42)
Liquorice black and Christmas red food colourings
Royal icing (see page 42)
Edible glue

Equipment

12cm (4¾ inch) oval plaque cutter
8cm (3¼ inch) long Easter egg mould or 185g (6oz) sugarpaste (ready-to-roll icing)
4.5cm (1¾ inch) oval cutter
1.5cm (⅝ inch) and 1.75cm (¾ inch) round cutters
Dresden tool
Greaseproof paper (parchment) piping bag
Nos. 0, 1 and 2 piping tubes (tips)
3cm (1¼ inch) heart cutter
Ball tool

Base

1 Colour 45g (1½oz) mexican paste/pastillage dark grey with black food colouring, and cut out a 12cm (4¾ inch) oval plaque. Allow to dry.

Car body

2 If you do not have an egg mould, shape the sugarpaste into a half-egg shape of similar length, and allow to dry.

3 Colour 60g (2oz) paste red and roll out to a thin sheet. Place the egg mould or sugarpaste mould on the paste and cut round it to make an oval plaque the same size as the egg mould. Allow to dry.

4 Roll a thin sheet of red paste, drape it over the egg mould or sugarpaste mould and trim. Cut a section out of the top using the smaller oval cutter. Press the 1.75cm (¾ inch) round cutter on each side of the car body to give the impression of the doors. Allow to dry and remove from the mould.

Car details

5 From 30g (1oz) grey paste, mould the base of the seat and score with the veiner end of the dresden tool. Roll a thin piece for the back of the seat and shape the top edge with the small oval cutter. Cut a thin section, again shaped with the oval cutter, to form the dashboard. Attach the seat sections to the red base of the car and the dashboard to the body using royal icing in a greaseproof paper piping bag fitted with a no. 1 piping tube. Pipe a line to give the impression of the boot (trunk). Fix the body on to the red, egg-shaped base with royal icing and a no. 2 piping tube.

6 From 60g (2oz) black paste, cut a 9mm (⅜ inch) deep block, attach it to the grey base plaque and fix the car body on top.

> **7** Cut a red heart for the bonnet (hood) and fix in position. Roll a 5cm (2 inch) cylinder of black paste, tapered at each end. Mark a line down the centre with the veining end of the dresden tool and fix on for the folded-down roof.

> **8** Using red paste, roll a 12.5cm (4¾ inch) cylinder tapered about two-thirds of the way along, so that it is thinner in the centre with a bulb at each end. Flatten and fix to the side of the car for the wings and running board. Repeat on the other side of the car.

> **9** Roll thin cylinders of grey paste for the bumpers (fenders). Roll two small cones of red paste and make a depression in the blunt end of each with the ball tool. Flatten a small ball of grey paste into each depression to complete the headlamps. Attach to the front wings.

> **10** Cut five discs of white paste using the small round cutter, and allow to dry. Cut five discs of black paste using the larger round cutter, and press the smaller discs into the centre. Four of these are used for the wheels; the fifth is for the steering wheel.

> **11** Pipe spokes on the wheels and steering wheel, and pipe on the door handles, the rear lights and the centre line of the bonnet using grey royal icing and a no. 0 piping tube. Attach the wheels and steering wheel to complete.

Birthday cake

> **1** From 30g (1oz) dark brown paste, mould a cone for the body of the bear and two cylinders for the arms. Trim the base off the cone and attach the arms, making a depression in the end of each.

> **2** Make the scarf from a flattened disc of white paste scored with the dresden tool.

> **3** Mould the head of the bear as for the bears' heads on the Child's Teddy Card (see page 32).

> **4** Roll two cones of honey-coloured paste and mark the blunt ends into fingers. Fix on to the arms.

> **5** Trim the wrists and front of the jacket with white paste.

6 Position the bear in the car, and fix the ornament on top of the cake. Instructions for making the other decorations on the cake are given on page 44.

You've passed your test

1 Make the bear as above. Cut two small squares of white paste and allow to dry, then paint an 'L' on each. Attach to the plaque at the rear of the car, as if they have just been removed from the car and tossed aside!

Bon voyage

1 Make the bear as above. Mould a suitcase from 15g (½oz) dark brown paste and place next to the driver.

Wedding car

1 Make two bears, one as above with a top hat, the other in white with a veil.

2 Mould small cans from grey paste and fix to the plaque, piping a line with royal icing and a no. 0 piping tube to attach the cans to the back of the car.

3 Cut a rectangle of paste and allow to dry, then paint 'Just Married' on to it. Attach to the back of the car.

4 Using a tiny heart plunger cutter, cut out a few hearts and place on the car, bride and groom for confetti.

Basic Recipes

Mexican Paste

This paste is easier to make than pastillage and can be used immediately. Do not use too much cornflour when rolling out as this might cause the paste to crack. Keep the paste covered at all times. The paste should keep at room temperature for about 6 weeks. It can also be frozen and will only take a short time to thaw. It is ideal for plaques, sheet work (such as cards), modelling and even flowers.

1 teaspoon liquid glucose
250g (8oz) icing (confectioner's) sugar
3 teaspoons gum tragacanth or CMC (compound – gum tragacanth substituté)
6 teaspoons cold water

1 Warm the liquid glucose, and place in a bowl with all the other ingredients. Knead or mix until you have a stiff dough.

2 Alternatively, place all the ingredients, except the water, in the bowl of a food processor or mixer, turn on the machine and gradually add the water until the mixture forms a ball. This takes about 40 seconds. (The mixture will be quite warm because of the speed of the machine, if using a processor.)

3 Place the paste in a strong plastic food bag and then in an airtight container. Either use at once or keep at room temperature.

Royal Icing

When using royal icing, keep the container covered with a damp cloth to prevent a crust forming. Any leftover icing should be put in an airtight container with a piece of plastic wrap pressed on to the surface of the icing to prevent a crust forming. Store in the fridge and re-beat before use.

5–8 tablespoons cold water
2 tablespoons Meri white (egg white albumen or substitute)
500g (1lb) icing (confectioner's) sugar

1 Either mix by hand, or use a food mixer on slow speed (easier and quicker). Gradually add 5 tablespoons water to the Meri white or substitute, and stir. Add the sugar and mix until the icing stands in firm peaks, adding more water if necessary.

Variation

By adding 25g (¾ oz) Tylo powder to 500g (1lb) royal icing you can produce another modelling paste. This can be used for similar work as mexican paste but it is a little softer and you can continue working with it a little longer.

Pastillage

Store pastillage in an airtight container to mature for at least 24 hours before using. The paste can be frozen.

3 tablespoons cold water
1½ teaspoons powdered gelatine
500g (1lb) icing (confectioner's) sugar
½ teaspoon gum tragacanth or CMC (compound – gum tragacanth substitute)

1 Put the water in a small heatproof bowl and sprinkle over the gelatine. Leave to soak for about 5 minutes or until the gelatine softens and becomes sponge-like.

2 Warm a mixing bowl, then put in it the sugar and gum tragacanth or CMC. (Warming the bowl is important – if the sugar is too cold, the gelatine will set in small lumps or 'spots'.)

3 Put the gelatine over a saucepan of hot water (or for a few seconds in the microwave) until completely dissolved. Do not boil the mixture.

4 Pour the gelatine solution into the warmed bowl containing the other dry ingredients, and knead until a smooth dough is formed.

Cake Ideas

A selection of cakes has been used to give ideas on how best to present the cake ornaments. Below are brief notes on how each cake was constructed.

Covering Cakes

Cakes are brushed with apricot glaze and coated with marzipan (almond paste). After drying, the marzipan is brushed with alcohol or boiled water and covered with sugarpaste (ready-to-roll icing).

Christmas Cake
(page 25)

1 Pipe a shell border around the base of the cake using royal icing in a greaseproof paper piping bag fitted with a no. 42 piping tube. Cut out four round sections from the side of the cake using a 4cm (1½ inch) round cutter. Make four plaques using the same cutter, attaching a pastillage stocking to two of them and two pastillage parcels decorated with red royal icing and a no. 0 piping tube to the other two. Fix in place in the cut-out sections of the cake.

2 Make wreaths by cutting a 4.5cm (1¾ inch) disc and removing the centre with a 4cm (1½ inch) cutter. Pipe green royal icing using a no. 42 piping tube and stipple. Allow to dry, then dust with brown and green dusting powders and attach

white plunger blossoms for the roses. Paint the centres yellow. Add red ribbons and bows (see page 30). Attach to the cake with royal icing.

Fathers Day Cake
(page 29)

1 Make the ribbons and bows for the side designs as described for the Child's

Teddy Card on page 30. Twist and attach the ribbons in loose circles on the side of the cake.

2 Fix a modelled bottle or parcel inside each circle of ribbon. Instructions for making these are given on page 28.

43

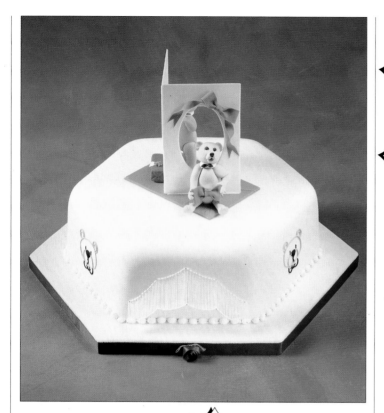

Convertible Car Cake
(page 41)

1 Pipe a shell border around the base of the cake using royal icing in a greaseproof paper piping bag fitted with a no. 42 piping tube.

2 Make four plaques from pale blue pastillage, using a 4.5cm (1¾ inch) round cutter. Cover the lower half of each plaque with a thin piece of grey pastillage to represent the road. Using grey, red, dark brown, black and dark brown/egg yellow paste, assemble the bas relief bear driving the car. Remember, when building up bas relief pieces, start with the section that appears furthest away from the eye. In this case, make the top half of the bear's body and scarf, then the bear's head (ears first), followed by the body of the car. Add the wings, head-lamps and bumpers last and finally pipe a red heart on the bonnet of each car using a no. 0 piping tube.

3 Fix the plaques to the side of the cake with royal icing. The milestones are made

Child's Teddy Card Cake
(page 31)

1 Pipe a shell border around the base of the cake using royal icing in a greaseproof paper piping bag fitted with a no. 42 piping tube. At the base of each shell, pipe a small bulb of claret icing using a no. 0 tube.

2 On alternate sides of the hexagon cake, pipe float-ing extension work using a no. 0 piping tube. Using the same tube, pipe a picot dot border around the top edge of the extension work. Finish off by piping small bulbs of claret icing on the picot edging and along the bridge of the extension work.

3 On the remaining sides of the cake, using dark brown/egg yellow coloured icing, pipe the head of the bear using a no. 0 piping tube. Pipe the eyes and the bow-tie using a no. 1 piping tube and black royal icing, finally flooding the nose with thinned down black royal icing.

4 The board is trimmed with claret-coloured ribbon and a matching ribbon rose secured in position with a pin through the centre. This pro-vides an attractive edge decora-tion as well as neatly covering the join in the ribbon.

from flattened pieces of grey pastillage with the inscription painted on with a fine brush (no. 2) and black food colouring once dry. The grass round the base is green pastillage textured using the veining end of a dresden tool.

Wheelbarrow Cake
(page 11)

1 ▷ Pipe a shell border around the base of the cake using royal icing in a greaseproof paper piping bag fitted with a no. 42 piping tube.

2 ▷ At the base of each side, attach a cauliflower with two carrots on either side, made as described for the wheelbarrow cake top (see page 12).

Christening Cake
(page 37)

1 ▷ Pipe a shell border around the base of the cake using royal icing in a greaseproof paper piping bag fitted with a no. 42 piping tube. Make six plaques from pastillage using a 4.5cm (1¾ inch) round cutter.

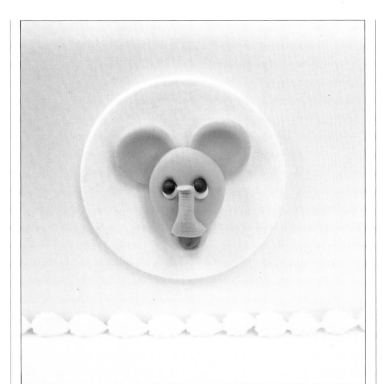

2 ▷ Cut small squares of yellow, green and blue pastillage, and fix one of each colour on to one of the plaques to represent building blocks. Repeat on a second plaque.

3 ▷ For the dog, make the ears from a cylinder of brown paste and fix in a curve to the plaque. Form a flat cone of pale brown paste for the head and attach to the plaque, point downwards, so it slightly overlaps the ears. Lift the tip of the nose up and add a small ball of black paste. Make two depressions for the eye sockets and complete the eyes with black paste. Make a lower jaw from a small disc of pale brown paste. Repeat on a second plaque.

4 ▷ The elephant is formed from two discs of grey paste for the ears and a flattened cone fixed point downwards for the head. Make a depression in the tip of the cone and attach a small piece of red paste for the tongue. The trunk is a cylinder of grey paste scored with a knife and pinched at the end between finger and thumb. Repeat on a second plaque.

5 ▷ Fix the plaques to the sides of the cake using royal icing.

Templates

Mouse Valentine Plaque (page 17)

Bunny Valentine Plaque (page 19)

Wishing Well (page 14)
roof end section

Wishing Well (page 14)
base outline

Wheelbarrow
(page 10)
gloves

Wheelbarrow
(page 10)

x2

x2

x1

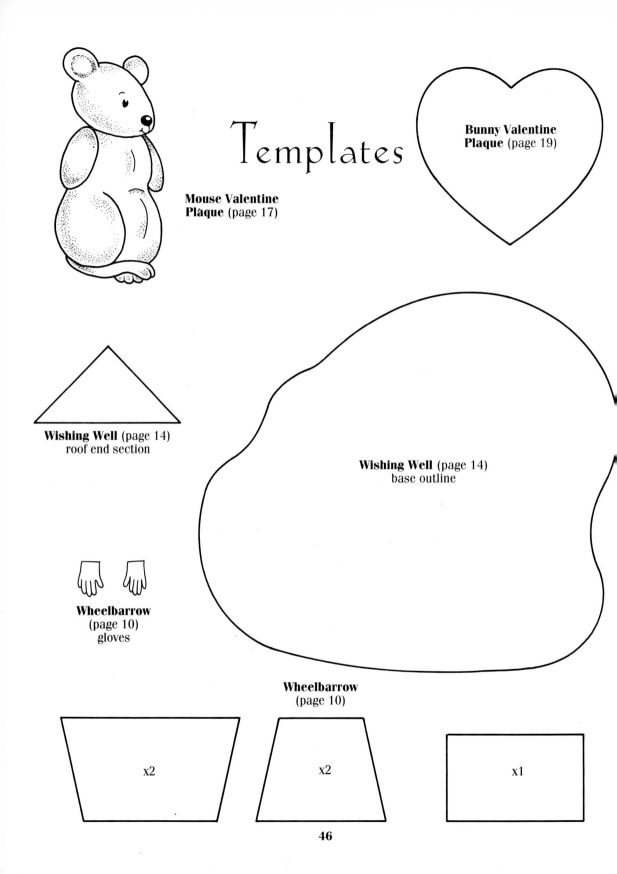

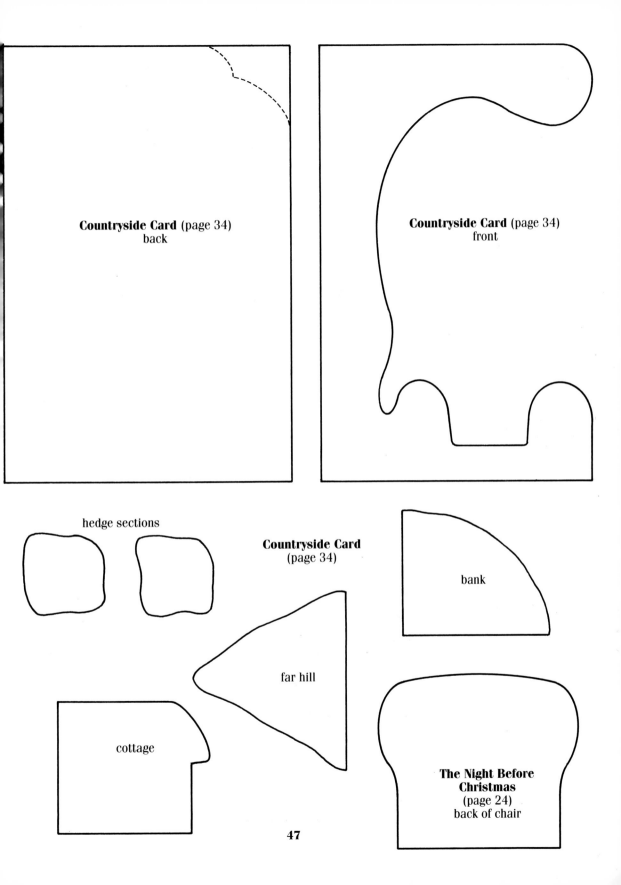

Countryside Card (page 34)
back

Countryside Card (page 34)
front

hedge sections

Countryside Card
(page 34)

bank

far hill

cottage

**The Night Before
Christmas**
(page 24)
back of chair

Acknowledgements

The publisher would like to thank the following suppliers:

Anniversary House (Cake Decorations) Ltd
Unit 16,
Elliott Road,
West Howe Industrial Estate,
Bournemouth,
Hampshire BH11 8LZ

Cake Art Ltd
Venture Way,
Crown Estate,
Priorswood,
Taunton,
Devon TA2 8DE

Guy, Paul and Co. Ltd
Unit B4,
Foundry Way,
Little End Road,
Eaton Socon,
Cambridgeshire PE19 3JH

J F Renshaw Ltd
(for supplying Regalice and Regalmarz)
Crown Street,
Liverpool L8 7RF

Squires Kitchen
Squires House,
3 Waverley Lane,
Farnham,
Surrey GU9 8BB